Singles and Doubles Tennis Strategies

By Joseph Correa

The best strategies professional players use!

COPYRIGHT PAGE

This book is dedicated to my family for always being there no matter what the situation.

INTRODUCTION

The importance of strategic tennis can be seen often in competitive tennis and knowing how to apply those strategies can help win more matches against tougher opponents. These strategies will allow you to do three things:

1. Prepare for a specific style of player.

2. You will know what counter strategies can be used to most effectively compete.

3. How to execute those strategies based on your style of play.

Being successful in singles or doubles requires that be prepared to excel against any type of playing style and that you are able to adapted quickly and effectively to overcome them.

The best tennis players in the world do this on a daily basis because that's the only for them to succeed and you can too with these strategies.

This tennis strategy playbook is pocket size and should be kept in your tennis bag or where you will most likely see it to keep you ready to apply which ever strategy will be most useful for that match.

ABOUT THE AUTHOR

Joseph Correa is a professional tennis player and coach that has competed and taught all over the world in ITF and ATP tournaments for many years. Besides being a professional tennis player he has a USPTR professional coaching certification and ITF kids coaching certification and has coached hundreds of tennis players.

As the author of this book, I firmly believe in the importance of implementing Specific strategies in tennis. Sometimes a better player can lose to a lower level player simply because of using the wrong strategy and the other way around. This book will help you win more matches and give your more success in your tennis life.

Best wishes,

Joseph Correa

CONTENT

CHAPTER 3: AGAINST ADVANCED STYLES OF SINGLES PLAY

CHAPTER 4: AGAINST UNUSUAL STYLES OF SINGLES PLAY

15. How to beat the grunter

16. How to beat the time delaying player

17. How to overcome a fast paced player

18. How to beat the crowd favorite

19. How to counter soft angles

20. How to counter deep and high shots

21. How to counter overcome high backhands

22. How to beat the scrap shot player

CHAPTER 5: MENTAL SINGLES AND DOUBLES STRATEGIES

23. How to overcome nerves

24. How to overcome stress in a match

25. How to stay focused until the end

26. What to think during change-overs

27. What to think before a match

28. What to think the night before a match

29. What to do when you're a set down

30. What to do when you are a set up

31. What to do when you have match point

32. What to do after serving a double fault

CHAPTER 1: DOUBLES STYLES OF PLAY

Strategy #1

How to beat the doubles baseline players

PROBLEM:

Doubles baseline players are known for not starting or coming to the net. They will come to the net as little as possible because their strength is on the baseline. They are often difficult opponents because there is no fast way to win points.

SOLUTION:

One of the best ways to defeat a baseline doubles team is to either come into the net as a team or to make the other team come into the net to get them out of their comfort zone.

The best ways to beat this type of doubles strategy is to:

- Play your normal style of play and not mind what your opponents are doing.

- Rush the net as a team to create a wall in front of the singles players so that they have to take some form of risk and make some errors which is what you want them to do.

- Come into the net with short slices down the middle of the court which can confuse many doubles teams specially when they are both on the back court and will have to decide who goes forward to hit that ball which often delays their reaction time.

- Hit a drop shot and bring them into the net so that at least one of them has to get out of the baseline and thus breaking their doubles structure. The drop will be most effective if it is hit into the center of the court because it will require that they decide who will run for it and this usually slows their reaction time and making it a more effective strategy.

Strategy #2

How to beat the serve and volley doubles team

PROBLEM:

The serve and volley team and are the most common style of play and the most classic as well. One player will start at the net while the other will serve and run to the net to volley. They will do this consistently on every point.

SOLUTION:

The best approach against this style of play is to focus and minimizing your errors on return of serve. The best ways to do this and beat a serve and volley doubles team is to:

- Keep your return of serve low and at their feet when they are coming into the net.

- Lob the net person often to break their structure of play and get them both to have to scramble in position and out of place.

- Surprise the net person by returning down the line in case they are poaching consistently.

Strategy #3

How to overcome the master poachers

PROBLEM:

Master poachers or a doubles team where the net person cuts off a shot intended for the baseline person and finishes that point at the net are very aggressive but still very beatable. This style of play is also very common and complements the classic one person at the net and one person on the back court doubles team.

SOLUTION:

Master poachers can be very imposing if your partner hits slow or mid-height ground strokes when they are rallying back and forth with the other doubles baseline person. The best way the out play this style of double team is to make sure you keep the net person from hitting balls as often as possible. You can do this by:

- Hitting short angled cross court shots.

- Hitting lobs over the net person.

- Hitting hard fast shots straight at their body so that they don't try to poach as often. Do this only if you feel comfortable doing this and feel it is necessary.

Strategy #4

What to do against the "I" formation doubles team

PROBLEM:

The "I" formation doubles team is a more advanced style of doubles team. One person stands to serve as close to the center of the court as possible and the net person kneels on one knee and stands in the center of the net as low as possible as to jump up once the serve is hit. The person serving will normally serve down the middle or to the center of the court. Sometimes they will serve at the body as well to change things up. The doubles team will decide in advance to which side the net person will go to, either the right or the left and sometimes simple hover in the middle. They stand in an "I" formation as to become unpredictable to their opponents

SOLUTION:

To overcome this type of doubles team you have to understand that you will not always guess right but you can take the necessary steps to be in the best position to win the point. The right shots to hit against an "I" formation doubles team will be:

- Lob down the line as to keep the ball away from the net person and break up their formation.

- Return serve straight down the middle low at the person at the net. The ball has to be hit hard or else the net person will have an easy volley.

- Choose one side and return serve there. Decide before hitting the return of serve as the net person can be very distracting and will make you take your eyes off the ball.

Strategy 5

What to do against the aggressive doubles net player

PROBLEM:

The aggressive doubles net player will be all over the net hitting winning shots often and putting pressure on their opponents to hit passing shots. These are great doubles partners to have because they get you lots of free points and put you in a winning position often.

SOLUTION:

Aggressive doubles net players have to be slowed down or at least keep them away from the ball for the majority of the point. The 5 most effective options to do this are:

a) Lob the net person down the line

b) Hit low crosscourt angles with slice or topspin

c) Hit the net person at the body

d) Surprise the net person with fast and low down the line shots

e) Lob the net person crosscourt

Strategy #6

What to do against the high lobbing doubles team

PROBLEM:

A high lobbing doubles team will hit high deep lobs over and over trying to get you to over hit and miss an overhead. They are not going to hit winners. They are simply trying to get you to beat yourself. The match will be long and tiring for you if you don't know how to approach this style of play.

SOLUTION:

This type of doubles team will not make many errors and for this reason you have to be more strategic than them. You have to decide if can beat them at their game or if playing your own game is a better option. If you can out-lob them and win the match, then do so. If you want to try beating them with a more tactical approach you would begin by doing what you have to do to get them out of the baseline area. Hitting a drop shot from a high lob is very difficult and even if you get it done, it will probably be very weak and easy to put away.

The best way to beat this style of play is to hit short angles as to pull them forward and out wide. Short slice or topspin angles will normally not get to the baseline and will definitely be much harder to hit a good lob from. Once you hit a short angle you want to quickly hit behind the person who just returned the angled shot so that they have to hit a weak reply. They reply and be countered by attacking the net and hitting down the middle or to an angle where they will not be able to hit a decent lob.

Strategy #7

How to break serve in serve in doubles

PROBLEM:

Breaking serve in doubles is important and necessary to win often. Sometimes you might play a very good serving team and other times they might have weak serves but difficult to attack because of the spin or height at which they arrive.

SOLUTION:

To break serve in doubles you need to make sure you don't over hit and be as consistent as possible. Try this when returning serve:

- Don't go for low percentage shots that land near the line and will probably be returned any way.

- Focus on a place on the court where you want to return serve. Usually the middle of the open court is a good starting place.

- Keep your backswing short and follow through your stroke.

- Don't hit too soft or too hard. Find a mid-ground in terms of power so that you don't become overly cautious nor overly aggressive.

- Keep your eyes on the ball not on the net person.

- Focus on moving your feet before returning serve so that you don't get flat footed.

- Stand in the appropriate place to return serve according to where your opponent is standing to serve.

Strategy #8

How to hold serve in doubles

PROBLEM:

Holding serve in doubles requires a team effort but can be done consistently regardless of power, height, and age. Most people try to go for too many big serves or big shots to win points but tennis is won through the sum of points not because of one big shot. That's an important point to remember for any strategy.

SOLUTION:

Holding serve requires that you have a plan and then execute that plan as a team. This has to be very clear or else find another doubles partner. You are not two separate people playing on one side. You are a team and must move, work, and think as a team. To hold serve in doubles you should:

- Get as many first serves in a possible. This might require that you take some power off your serve or go for fewer corners or lines. This will minimize the risk of having your opponents attack a weak second serve which is vital in order to hold serve.

- Always get the first ball in after your opponent has returned serve. Too many people try to do too much with that first shot which often results in unforced errors which quickly add up.

- Work your way through the point. Sometimes this may mean that you will want to get to the net after hitting the right shot and not just any shot.

- Make sure that you both decide in advance (and not in the middle of the point) who will cover the middle of the court if a ball is hit their since this a very easy way for your opponents to get points.

CHAPTER 2: AGAINST BASIC STYLES OF SINGLES PLAY

Strategy #1

How to beat the baseliner

PROBLEM:

A good baseliner is comfortable at the baseline and would prefer not to go to the net. For this reason, the best strategy would be to bring the baseliner to the net with defensive shots where they will be in the worst situation and will probably get based or simply miss an easy volley.

SOLUTION:

One of the best ways to defeat a baseliner is to bring them into the net by hitting any of these shots: a short slice, a drop shot, a short topspin, a short angle.

If you hit a short slice the baseliner will be tempted to come into the net and if it's very short, he should be forced to leave the baseline and come forward to do a volley or overhead.

If you hit a drop shot, you will definitely be able to bring your opponent into the net as they will have no choice but to step inside the serving boxes at the net.

If you hit a short topspin shot, they won't be forced to come into the net but will be in a very bad position on the court if they don't. You can take advantage of their bad positioning by simply hitting behind them.

If you hit a short angle, they not only will be off the baseline but also slightly out of the court which would put them in a very bad position if they don't try to cover the court by coming into the net.

If you have a good serve, serve and volley or rush the net simply to surprise them and get some free errors every once in a while.

Strategy #2

What to do against a net-rusher

PROBLEM:

The net rusher is always ready to move forward mostly on second serves, weak shots and short balls. Their best shots are normally their volleys and overhead. They will rush the net after serving as well. They win most points by putting pressure at the net which forces errors or bad decisions from opponents.

SOLUTION:

The best solutions is to simply keep the net-rusher on the baseline by getting your first serve in, even of that means taking some power off and placing the ball instead. Also, hit deep topspin and cross-court to keep the net-rusher out of the court and away from the net. If the net-rusher has reached the net you should plan to:

1. Pass them by hitting down the line.

2. Pass them by hitting crosscourt.

3. Pass them by hitting a short angle.

4. Lob the ball over their backhand side with a flat, topspin or slice shot.

5. Hit the ball straight at their body to keep them off guard and slow them down.

Strategy #3

How to beat the counter-puncher

PROBLEM:

The counter-puncher is not the one to take the initiative during the point. They are usually the type of players that will wait for you to make a decision and then out-do your shot. If you rush the net they will pass you. If you attack by hitting harder they will use your power and play the open court. These types of players are big trouble when you don't know how to play them. The harder and faster you play the better it is for them if you don't have a concise strategy.

SOLUTION:

To beat the counter-puncher you need to understand that most of the time if you want to attack, you need to make sure you have a pattern beforehand that you can put into practice during the point. A few examples would be:

- Serve out wide and then hit to the open court.

- Hit to the open court and then follow your shot to the net to put more pressure on your opponent and close out the point.

- Hit a short ball and force them to take the initiative by coming into the net.

Strategy #4

How to beat the serve and volley player

PROBLEM:

Serve and volley players are fast and decisive. They will not blink when they have the opportunity to finish the point. They will serve a strong serve with power or spin and then follow it to the net.

SOLUTION:

The best strategy against this style of play is to slow them down or stop them as they come in. The three best ways to slow them down and get them to make more errors are:

1. Return their serve to their feet so that they have to hit a half volley.

2. Return their serve right at their body as to make them have to turn their body out of the way to volley. This might not be a nice way to slow them down but it works and is another tool when you have no other options.

3. Lob them. Simply return the ball high and deep and then you should back up in case they decide to hit a hard overhead in the air as many will try to do this. If you hit a high enough lob they will have to stop completely and hit a well-timed overhead that is not always easy when it's windy, rainy, mid-day and the sun is right in their eyes or at night when it's most difficult to distinguish distances.

Strategy #5

How to out-play the all-court player

PROBLEM:

The all-court player can do it all. Serve and volley, counter-punch, chip and charge the net, be patient and consistent on the back court. Everyone is always practicing and working hard to become an all-court player so that you don't have any obvious weaknesses which would make it easier for you opponent to attack.

SOLUTION:

The all-court player is usually good at everything but that does not mean they don't have weaknesses. Focus on what they do worst and adjust the match so that you are doing what you do best.

For example: if they have a weaker backhand and you have a strong forehand, you should serve to their backhand and then run around your backhand as to hit a forehand. Continue putting pressure by hitting to their backhand until you get the opportunity to come to the net and or to put the ball away. This way you force them to play your most effective style of play against their weakest shot. Another good strategy would be to attack the net on their weaker side and force them to make errors this way.

Strategy #6

How to overcome the lobber

PROBLEM:

Players who lob the ball or hit high moon balls over and over again can be very difficult to play against and can make you lose your patience. You want to attack but they simply slow everything down with their lobs. When you want to come into the net you know you're going to have to hit an overhead.

SOLUTION:

You don't want to lose a match because you're going for low percentage shots while your opponent is hitting percentage shots such as lobs. They best plan would be to get them out of their comfort zone and force them to hit lobs from bad positions on the court or in locations that do not allow them to lob. By hitting low angled shots you will force lobbers to step out of the back court and to the sides which makes for a much harder lob since the distance to the backcourt is short than if they were standing far behind the baseline. Another way to get these types of players out of their lobbing game is to simply hit a short ball or drop shot as to bring them into the net. At the net you can either volley or hit an overhead, but no lobs! Another effective way to beat lobbers is to hit low short slices as it is much harder to hit a decent lob of a shot like that and then you can simply hit behind them after they return a not so good lob. The last option you have against a lobber is to hit the ball in the air so that the ball never bounces. This can be very effective if you're standing inside the baseline and feel comfortable swinging at balls in the air.

Strategy #7

How to beat a pusher

PROBLEM:

"Pushers" or consistent players who don't usually attack at all during the match are very successful a lot of times. They don't make very many errors and don't hit many winners either. They wait for you to make all the mistakes, which creates addition pressure on you.

SOLUTION:

"Pushers" usually need to be forced to make mistakes. One of the best ways to get them to make mistakes is by bringing them to the net with a drop shot or short ball and then simply making them volley or hit an overhead which is normally what they do worst since they spend so much time on the backcourt keeping the ball consistently in play. If you have a strong net game you should attack the net with fast, low shots forcing them to risk more by going for a passing shot or lob. Both strategies are effective against this style of play.

CHAPTER 3: AGAINST ADVANCED STYLES OF SINGLES PLAY

Strategy #8

What to do against a heavy topspin player

PROBLEM:

Heavy topspin is becoming more and more popular in today's game. It usually bounces up fast and high which makes it difficult to attack or come into the net. It will either force you to step back or move forward to hit the ball.

SOLUTION:

You can do several things to counter-attack heavy topspin balls. 1. You can simply step back and let the ball come down to a comfortable hitting position for you. This way you're not hitting at or above should height which is a much harder shot to hit for most people. 2. You can hit the ball as it's rising before it gets too high and step into the court as you do this. Doing this requires more skill then letting it come back down but it can be rewarding if you can keep your opponent rushed with you quick on-the-rise returns.

Strategy #9

How to overcome the slice-only player

PROBLEM:

Some tennis payers will only hit slice shots because they are either very successful doing this or because they don't know how to hit any other types of shots. The ball will stay low and short which makes it harder to attack or hit clean winners off.

SOLUTION:

Being patient with this type of player pays off in the long run. The key is not to over hit those low slices. Try to get low and move forward. The best way to get them to miss is by either, getting them on the run and then closing the net when they slice it back, or to mix up the heights on them. Mixing up heights basically means hitting a low topspin shot and then a high topspin shot and continuing to follow this pattern until they don't find the correct angle on their racquet forcing them to hit too low at the net or too high and out.

Strategy #10

How to return a big serve

PROBLEM:

Big servers are tough opponents because of the speed at which the ball comes at you. The ball will come hard and fast, without much warning.

SOLUTION:

Keep a short back swing and move your feet before the ball comes. Make to split-step when they are impacting the ball as to improve your reaction time. The secret to returning fast serves is not to over hit. Learn to use your opponent's power by simply returning a well-placed ball. A lot of times you will noticed that you don't need to hit the ball harder for it to be a good return and that's the most important thing to remember. Move your feet, keep your eyes on the ball, take a short back swing, and move forward as you hit the ball to have success with this shot.

Strategy #11

How to counter a drop shot

PROBLEM:

Drop shots are great weapons to have since they don't require any power. It's a finesse shot or also known as a touch shot. Drop shots are just as valuable as hitting a winner or an overhead. Remember that the distance going side to side on the court is shorter than the distance moving forward to the net. When you hit a drop shot you actually make your opponent run a longer distance.

SOLUTION:

The best counter shot against a drop shot is simply to hit another drop shot back. This way you have a lesser chance of getting passed or lobbed or even getting aimed at. If can master this shot, you will make more than one opponent struggle running forward for a shot they did not expect. The second shot you can hit against a drop shot is a deep return to your opponent's weaker side and then simply expect to hit a volley or overhead. If you want to reduce the amount of drop shots your opponent hit to you, you can either hit the ball hard and deep or keep the ball high and deep. This will make it a lot harder for them to hit a drop shot.

Strategy #12

How to overcome the runner

PROBLEM:

Runners are tough adversaries because they normally don't give up and they get many balls back in play. Some players win their matches with sheer speed. They chase ball after ball until their opponents end up going for too much and finally miss.

SOLUTION:

Runners always have a weaker shot. It could be their backhand, forehand, serve, volleys, or overhead. Find their weakest shot and start attacking that shot instead of going for winners. You have to understand that their biggest strength is their speed so you have to focus on what they do worst even though that means not hitting clean winners. You have to be patient and allow them to make the mistakes with their weakest shot. Insist and be persistent until they start making errors with that shot and then don't deviate from the plan. You'll be tempted to finish the point but it always pays to stick with the plan instead of allowing your opponent to do what they do best, which is run down balls. To beat these types of players attack their weaknesses, not their speed since that's where you will end up working the hardest to win points. Stick with the plan and be persistent.

Strategy #13

How to out-play a big forehand

PROBLEM:

Big or power forehands are common in tennis as everyone has to have weapons in order to win points and more often than not, their forehands are their strongest shots. In today's game power forehands have become a necessity to win more points as players get faster and stronger which means the ball needs to go faster and harder if you want to get past them.

SOLUTION:

Big forehands are big as long as they are being hit in their power zones, which is normally between the knees and shoulder height. If you can make them hit shots below the height of their knees and above the height of their shoulders, chances are their forehands won't be as big any more. Try hitting low slices to their forehand or high topspin to reduce the amount of power they can generate off that side.

Strategy #14

How to overcome a big hitter

PROBLEM:

Big hitters overpower their opponents off both wings and can often start points with a blazing serve. They win points by simply hitting harder than others.

SOLUTION:

You need to slow down big hitters with some off-speed shots like: slow slices, side-slices, high topspin, deep balls, drop shots and short angles. Big hitters hate changes in ball speeds because it forces them to have to adjust to the depth, height and speed the ball. After a while these changes in speed, spin, and height make big hitters either miss or have to slow down to reduce their errors. That when you know you got them out of their game plan and now you can start winning more points.

CHAPTER 4: AGAINST UNSUAL STYLES OF SINGLES PLAY

Strategy #15

How to beat the "grunter"

PROBLEM:

The "grunter" can be loud and distracting. They will grunt every time they hit the ball and will increase the loudness of the grunt depending on the length of the point, importance of the point, or on how tired they are.

SOLUTION:

Learn to focus on the more important aspects of your game like breathing and footwork. Focusing too much on what your opponent is doing will distract you and keep you away from playing your best tennis. Find things that you can focus on in between point like: fixing your strings, tying your shoe strings if they are untied or loose, toweling off when you're sweaty. If it's too much distraction for you, simply grunt as well.

Strategy #16

How to beat the time-delaying player

PROBLEM:

Players who intentional delay time between points and change-overs are looking to control the tempo of the match. Some players need to play fast in order to maintain them tempo while others don't mind playing slower. Slowing down a match when you're losing is a great strategy as it gives you more time to fix any mistakes your making and get back on track. When someone does this to you it can be difficult to find your game again.

SOLUTION:

Focus on what you need to be doing. Don't fall into their trap by delaying the match. Simply stand ready every time and show them that you are ready to go.

Strategy #17

How to overcome a fast paced player

PROBLEM:

Some players like to rush through points, not allowing their opponents to take their time and think things through which causes more errors if you're not used to being rushed. They usually take short water breaks and are always starting to serve before you get to the baseline to return serve.

SOLUTION:

When someone is constantly rushing play, the best plan is to simply slow things down to where you feel comfortable and know you won't make errors due to being rushed. Some of the best ways to accomplish this are:

- Toweling off, drinking water and breathing slowly during change-overs.

- Putting your towel on the back or side fence in between points as to have to walk to dry off with your towel and slow down play.

- Tying your shoe strings before serving or before returning serve.

  - Fixing your racquet strings before serving or before returning serve.

Strategy #18

How to beat the crowd favorite

PROBLEM:

Crowd favorite players can have quite a following during points. Some crowds and family members can very loud and intense which makes it hard for anyone to focus on the match. They clap when you lose a point. They clap on important points and in the middle of rallies.

SOLUTION:

Crowd favorites are difficult opponents when they are winning but when they are losing things get quite. Concentrate on beginning the match winning and stay on top. The bigger the lead you have, the less noise you will hear from the crowd. Some of their fans, family members, and other people will simply leave the match which will mean less distraction for you and better results. If you're the type of player that actually enjoys having a crowd against you while competing, then I would still recommend that you start winning and continue to stay on top until the match is over. Crowd favorites are only favorites while they are winning or at least have a chance at winning but if you can prove they have no chance, and then you will have a much easier time.

Strategy #19

How to counter soft angles

PROBLEM:

Soft angles are great weapons to have because they force players to step off the baseline and into the front and side court. This opens up the entire court for your opponent and practically allows them to have almost full control of the point.

SOLUTION:

The best way to counter a soft angled shot is to do one of three things:

- Follow the ball to the net and cut off the angle that was just created.

- Return another angle crosscourt and step back into the middle of the court.

- Hit a drop shot right in front of you as to bring your opponent to the net and then cover the middle of the court to block any possibility of a passing shot.

Strategy #20

How to counter deep and high shots

PROBLEM:

Deep high shots, if done consistently, will cause many errors from most tennis players. They basically push you far back behind the baseline and they force you to hit falling back which reduces the amount of power you can generate on your next shot. Even they are done with or without topspin; they still represent a threat and require a good counter-attack.

SOLUTION:

Deep high shots can be countered in a number of ways.

- You can step back and return another high deep shot and how your opponent reacts to this shot.

- You can hit it on the rise as soon as the ball bounces.

- You can slice the ball back to keep the ball low and short.

  Besides countering their high deep shots, you can also prevent them from hitting this type of shot by:

- Hitting low angled slice or topspin strokes.

- Catching the ball in the air by hitting a volley or swinging volley to keep the ball from landing deep.

- **Slicing low short shots that force your opponent to step into the court and make it much more difficult for them to hit another accurate high deep shot.**

Strategy #21

How to overcome high backhands

PROBLEM:

High backhands are one of the most troublesome shots for most players, especially if you have a one-handed backhand. High backhands require more strength to bring back into the court and backhands normally are not the ones to hit the best high shots with.

SOLUTION:

You can overcome high backhands in three ways:

1. You can run around your backhand and hit a forehand.

2. You can hit your backhand on the rise before it becomes a high backhand.

3. You can step back as far as necessary as to hit a mid-height or low backhand again.

Strategy #22

How to beat the scrap-shot player

PROBLEM:

Scrap-shot players hit unorthodox balls with tricky spins and normally not very good technique but they get the ball in and don't make it easy to attack their shots. Some of the shots they usually hit are: slice, side-slice, side-topspin, moon balls, and drop shots that bounce and return to the net and soft touch shots.

SOLUTION:

When you don't know what to expect, the best solution is to stay on your toes and be prepared to hit all types of shots. Make sure you get close to the ball as it will move around more than usual. If you're not comfortable with the way the ball is bounce, attack the net where you will be hitting the ball in the air and not have to worry about how the ball bounces.

CHAPTER 5: MENTAL SINGLES AND DOUBLES STRATEGIES

Strategy #23

How to overcome nerves

PROBLEM:

Getting nervous during a tennis match is a natural reaction. The important thing is not letting your nerves get in the way of your performance. Sometimes being too nervous make you freeze during important points which force you to make silly mistakes or to increase your chances of missing.

SOLUTION:

There are a number of ways to overcome nerves. Here are just a few that work very well for most tennis players:

- Move your feet. A lot of times when you get nervous, you stop moving your feet which increases errors. Moving your feet more and quicker will help you to meet the ball better and will relax you during the point.

- Breathe during the point in and out. In as the balls comes to you and out as you impact the ball. When you are not playing the point it's even more important to breathe deeply to relax your muscles and help you focus on your strategy instead of what you're feel

- Lowering your intensity level. Try thinking positively about what you are planning to do during the point and breathing deeply and slowly to lower your heart rate.

Strategy #24

How to overcome stress in a match

PROBLEM:

Stress is another natural factor that occurs when you feel strained and under pressure to perform or by outside forces such as family, friends, being late, forgetting tennis equipment, weather conditions, etc.

SOLUTION:

To overcome stress you have to understand what is causes the stress in the first place. If you late to your match, you should make sure to take your time and not rush. You won't make up for lost time by going faster. That will actually promote more missed shots than anything else. If you're stressed about the weather and feel that it might start raining, you should focus on one point at a time and let the weather do what it will do regardless of what's going on in the match. If it's a family member, that's causing the stress, you should try to focus your attention on your match and block them from your mind if they are affecting your negatively. You can also ask them to please stay quiet during the match or to simply leave and come back after the match is done. Family members want you to be successful but the stress of the match can be too much for them. Focus on what is causing the stress and solve it so that you can focus on winning.

Strategy #25

How to stay focused until the end

PROBLEM:

Stay focused in your match until it's over is not an easy task since it requires hard work. Some people start good but finish terribly because of a lack of focus. Others never focus long enough to close a game or a set.

SOLUTION:

Staying focused during the entire match requires a few things.

1. You need to have visual reminders that will help you to keep your mind on what's most important to you in the match or what is helping you win more points. One of the best ways to do this is to have notes written down on a piece of paper that you can glance at during change-overs. This way you keep remembering what you need to be doing.

2. Write down on a sticker two or three important things that will help you stay focused in your match and place the sticker on a safe place on your racquet where it won't fall off. The inside of the neck of a tennis racquet is a great place to put a sticker. The neck of a tennis racquet is located between the grip and the strings.

Strategy #26

What to think during change-overs

PROBLEM:

Change-overs are one of the most underestimated times to think during a tennis match. What should you be thinking? You're tired and thirsty so why should you be thinking about anything? Well, change-overs are the best time to do what is most important in tennis and that is to think in order to find solutions to problems you're having in the match and finally succeed.

SOLUTION:

During change-overs you should be thinking about what is making you win points and what is making you lose points. If you're not winning points you should figure out why that is.

Maybe your opponent is taking control of the point from the start and forcing you to hit backhands only and not allowing you to use your forehand which might be your winning shot.

Maybe you're not moving your feet enough and need to start focusing on that.

Maybe your tired and want to win faster but don't know how but during the change-over you realize you need to be more aggressive and possible attack the net more or hit more drop shots.

Maybe your opponent isn't doing anything special and you're the one making all the errors. You realize this during the change-over and decide you need to start keeping the ball in play longer or force your opponent to make more mistakes.

Strategy #27

What to think before a match

PROBLEM:

Before the match it's important to think things through as to prepare a plan of attack but knowing what to think makes a big difference when it comes to winning and losing.

SOLUTION:

Yes, during the match you should do your best not to think too much but before the match you should definitely be preparing what you will be doing during the match so that you can go on "auto-pilot" during the match and simply execute what you thought of beforehand. You should be thinking about what you need to be doing be most successful. This could include:

- Moving your feet.

- Tossing the ball high on your serve.

- Following through on your ground strokes.

- Keep your eyes on the ball.

- Not rushing during points.

- To attack your opponents weakness right from the start.

- Attack your opponents' second serve.

- Not to let surroundings distract you.

Strategy #28

What to think the night before a match

PROBLEM:

The night before the match you should rest and think only about things you will have control over. Don't worry about things that won't benefit you in any way like rain, wind, etc. Make sure your body and mind rest the night before the match as you don't want to begin a new day tired or weak.

SOLUTION:

The night before the match you should practice visualizing how you would like to play the following day. You can imagine specific strategies you'd like to perform such as:

-   Slicing and attacking the net.

-   Hitting high topspin shots to your opponents backhand or weaker side.

-   Having long rallies crosscourt.

Other things you could be visualizing the night before could be:

-   Seeing you chase down difficult shots from corner to corner.

-   Standing confident to return serve.

- Tossing the ball proudly before serving.

- Being motivated and energetic in between points.

Strategy #29

What to do when you're a set down

PROBLEM:

When you're a set down you start doubting yourself and begin feeling you won't win the match. Know what to do to change things around is both emotional and physical.

SOLUTION:

When you are down a set you need to understand that the key is in knowing where it is that you're losing points and winning points.

If you're missing a lot of high shots and that's what your opponent if forcing you to hit most of the time, then you should try attacking the net more and reduce the amount of high shots you hit from the back court.

If you're losing long rallies because your fitness level isn't as strong as your opponents, then you should figure out a way to key points short. You could bring your opponent to the net more often or go for more winners.

If you're winning points when you run around your backhand and hit forehands, then you should try to run around as many shots and hit forehands.

If you won all the points where you made your first serve in, then you should focus on going for more first serves.

Strategy #30

What to do when you are a set up

PROBLEM:

If you won the first set, you have an emotional and psychological edge over in the match which weighs heavily. What should you do in the second set to win the match?

SOLUTION:

After winning the first set you know your opponent will make a greater effort to get on top in the score. Also, you know you're close to the finish line since you've already finished have the race.

The key is to do these 3 things:

1. Keep doing what you're doing to win points. Changing a winning strategy is not the right plan at this point. Don't make foolish changes by being less aggressive or more aggressive.

2. Make an extra effort for the first 3 games of the match so that you start with very good lead. This will demoralize your opponent and make the remainder of the match easier. 3-0 or 2-0 or 4-0 are all great starts to a second set.

3. Make sure you stay on top in the score until the match ends as to not let your opponent even consider they

have a chance at winning the match because if you don't do this, you will definitely regret it later on.

Strategy #31

What to do when you have match point

PROBLEM:

Match point can viewed in many different ways. Having the right approach makes all the difference. Being overconfident or doubting yourself are both very common but negative reactions to a match point. What you should you do?

SOLUTION:

Match point is the greatest opportunity in a match to win. Make sure you don't think too much during match point. Keep things simple. Whatever is making you win should be repeated during match point without a doubt and done with precision. If you get nervous, simply breathe and move your feet to get rid of some of the nerves. Don't look around or let yourself get distracted.

Remember: *STICK WITH THE ORIGINAL PLAN!*

Strategy #32

What to do after serving a double fault

PROBLEM:

Double faults affect you emotionally and psychologically. They are normal and can happen to you during a match as long as you don't do them too often. The difference is in what you do and think after you double fault to correct the situation.

SOLUTION:

Focus on what you need to do to get your serve in. Second serves require a higher degree of control because it's your last chance to get your serve in. Don't add any pressure to yourself or get nervous. Make sure your follow these 5 steps to double fault less:

1. Be selective with your tosses. Don't hit every toss. Take your time and only hit serves you feel will have a high chance of going in due to a well-placed toss.

2. Don't rush with your service motion.

3. Bounce the ball at least 4 times before serving as to slow you down.

4. Following through on your swing.

5. Keep your chin and head up when you impact the ball so that you can keep your eyes on the ball as long as possible.

Good luck in your matches and remember to use these strategies as often as possible. They will help you win more matches.

For more great tennis videos and books, check out tennisvideostore.com or on amazon.com.

MORE TITLES BY JOSEPH CORREA

Tennis Serve Harder Training Program

This DVD will teach you how to serve 10-20 mph faster in a 3 month day by day program. The best serve training program in the market. Video includes a 3 month chart training program and a step by step manual. The DVD shows you how to do the exercises properly and the process you should follow in order to be successful with the program.

Joseph Correa is a professional tennis player and coach that has competed and taught all over the world in ITF and ATP tournaments for many years. Besides being a professional tennis player he has a USPTR professional coaching certification and ITF kids coaching certification.

The 33 Laws of Tennis

The 33 Laws of Tennis is book full of valuable tennis concepts to help you become a better and more prepared tennis player. Written by a professional tennis player and coach in the USA. Its a very useful book that will come in handy when you least expect it and will remind you of many little but important things before competing.

Tennis Footwork and Cardio by Joseph Correa

Joseph Correa is a professional tennis player and coach that has competed and taught all over the world in ITF and ATP tournaments for many years. Besides being a professional tennis player he has a USPTR professional coaching certification and ITF kids coaching certification.

Get in better shape and improve your mobility on and off the tennis court. Your foot work will improve drastically as well as strengthen your core and upper body. Definitely worthwhile for a serious tennis player no matter what your level. You become faster, stronger, and more agile and on the court as well as seeing an increase in acceleration in your groundstrokes and serve. Created by a professional tennis player for others to advance in their game and win more matches.

Yoga Tennis by Joseph Correa

Yoga Tennis by Joseph Correa is a great way to improve your flexibility and agility on the court. Reach more balls and have less injuries. Its a great way to win more by working on a different part of your game. The DVD lasts about 30 minutes. Used by amateur and professional tennis players to improve their game and last longer in matches. This is the best way for a tennis player to become more flexible and get rid of common back, knee, shoulder, hamstring, calf, and quadriceps injuries. You'll be glad to got started! This is an improved version of our MBS Yoga Tennis 2012.

The Vilcabamba Diet

The best diet and exercise book you will find if you want to get in shape and live longer. Its based on a village in Ecuador called "Vilcabamba" where most of its inhabitants live longer than the average person and in great condition. A diet for exercise. Great for athletes!

Tennis Abs by Joseph Correa

Tennis Abs is a great way strengthen your core for more powerful serves, forehands and backhands as well as stronger volleys. Abs are key for a better game. This DVD works on many types of crunches, sit-ups, and lateral abs and back exercises that you won't find in other abdominal videos. Feel confident when changing your shirt during your match and hit the ball harder!

12 Tennis Secrets to Win More

By Joseph Correa

What you should be doing and working on to win all the time

32 Tennis Strategies For Today's Game

By Joseph Correa

Win more matches and tournaments with these valuable strategies for all levels!

54

TENNIS DRILLS

FOR TODAY'S GAME:

IMPROVE CONSISTENCY AND POWER

"This book will teach you how to become more consistent by adding spin to your shots which will give you the confidence to hit with more power."

By Joseph Correa

60

Tennis

Strategies

and

Mental Tactics:

Mental Toughness Training

By Joseph Correa

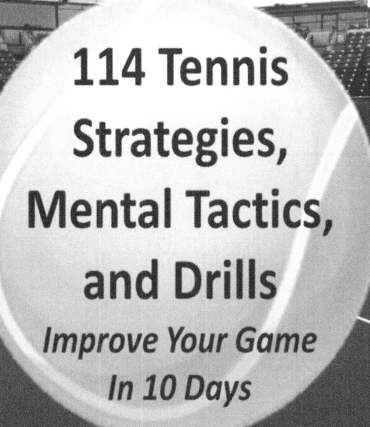

114 Tennis Strategies, Mental Tactics, and Drills

Improve Your Game In 10 Days

By Joseph Correa

AB TRAINING

By Joseph Correa©

Ab training for athletes of all levels!

1 DVD

Advanced

Tennis

Rope Drills

Learn how to hit with more topspin, depth, control, and precision than ever before!

By Joseph Correa

MBS

CARDIO TENNIS 2012©

By
Joseph Correa

This video includes intense
tennis training and abdominal
excercises that will dramatically
improve your speed and agility on court.

1 DVD

MBS

YOGA TENNIS 2012©

DVD
VIDEO

By
Joseph Correa

This video will improve your flexibility,
agility and balance on and off the court
with some awsome results.
Used by professional tennis players
and amateurs.

1 DVD

THE VILCABAMBA DIET

Learn how to live longer and healthier like the people of Vilcabamba!

This book includes:
101 Exercises You Can Do Any Time & Any Place plus BONUS ABS

By
Joseph G. Correa

In Collaboration With
Dr. Juan Carlos Correa

CARDIO TENNIS
AND ABS

BY JOSEPH CORREA©

1 DVD This video will improve your flexibility, agility and balance on and off the court with some awsome results. Used by professional tennis players and amateurs.

YOGA TENNIS
BY JOSEPH CORREA ©

This video will improve your flexibility, agility and balance on and off the court with some awsome results. Used by professional tennis players and amateurs.

1 DVD

Complete Tennis and Serve Conditioning by Joseph Correa

Improve your serve, foot speed, and agility with these videos that will get you winning more matches than ever before.

1 DVD

Tennis Fitness:

Tennis Abs, Yoga Tennis, and Serve Training

By Joseph Correa

Improve your serve, speed, and flexibility with this combination of footwork and stretches that will get you winning more matches than ever before.

1 DVD

Fit For Tennis:

Tennis Abs and Yoga Tennis

By Joseph Correa

Improve your serve, speed, and flexibility with this combination of footwork and stretches that will get you winning more matches than ever before.

1 DVD

Fit For Tennis:

Yoga Tennis, Serve Dynamics and Serve Training

By Joseph Correa

Improve your serve, speed, and flexibility with this combination of footwork and stretches that will get you winning more matches than ever before.

1 DVD

Fit For Tennis:

Yoga Tennis and Serve Training

By Joseph Correa

Improve your serve, speed, and flexibility with this combination of footwork and stretches that will get you winning more matches than ever before.

1 DVD

Les 33 Lois Du Tennis

Tennis

Par Joseph Correa

Comment améliorer votre jeu en trente trois concepts

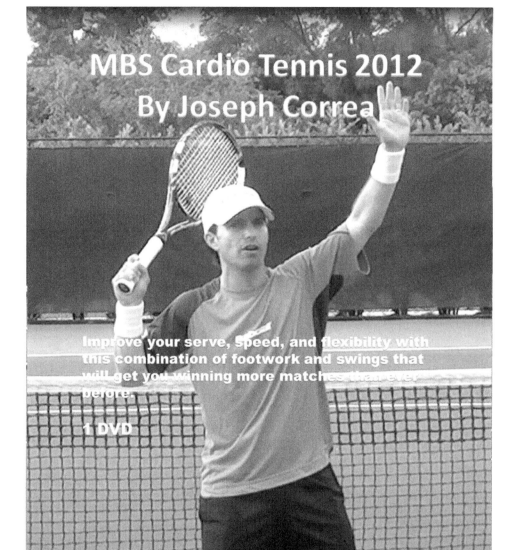

MBS Cardio Tennis 2012
By Joseph Correa

Improve your serve, speed, and flexibility with this combination of footwork and swings that will get you winning more matches than ever before.

1 DVD